from a 1610 map of Somerset

© Wooden Books Ltd 2007 AD

Published by Wooden Books Ltd.
8A Market Place, Glastonbury, Somerset

British Library Cataloguing in Publication Data
Wingfield, G.
Glastonbury, Isle of Avalon

A CIP catalogue record for this book is
available from the British Library

ISBN 978 1904263 19 7

Recycled paper throughout.
All rights reserved. For permission to
reproduce any part of this little bit of heaven
on earth please contact the publishers.

Printed and bound in Shanghai, China
by Shanghai iPrinting Co., Ltd.
100% recycled papers.

GLASTONBURY
ISLE OF AVALON

George Wingfield

This book is dedicated to my darling Jan

Many thanks to John Michell, Jamie George and Hamish Miller for their inspiration regarding the mysteries of Avalon. Thanks to Somerset Country Library, Bernard Chandler, to Dan Goodfellow for his artwork on pages 2, 5 & 52-57, and Mahmoud Drury for picture research.

Recommended reading: "New Light on the Ancient Mystery of Glastonbury" by John Michell, "The Isle of Avalon" by Nicholas Mann, "Glastonbury, Myth and Archaeology" by Philip Rahtz and Lorna Watts, "Glastonbury Abbey" by James Carley, "Glastonbury, Maker of Myths" by Frances Howard-Gordon and finally "The Sun and the Serpent" by Hamish Miller and Paul Broadhurst.

Pictures are mostly credited where they appear. Plates have been taken from Frederick Ross's 1882 "Ruined Abbeys" and William Stukeley's 1724 "Itinerarium Curiosum". While every effort has been made to contact image copyright holders, in some instances this has proved fruitless. If your work appears uncredited here, or you can help with unattributed pictures in any way, we aim to set things right in subsequent editions.

Above: Pomparles Bridge, connecting Glastonbury with Street, from which, misty legend has it, the sword Excalibur was thrown after King Arthur's burial on the Isle of Avalon.

CONTENTS

DOORWAY IN ST. JOSEPH'S CHAPEL.

INTRODUCTION

FEW WOULD GUESS that a small market town in Somerset was once considered the holiest ground in England. Its history, sanctity and the extraordinary origins of its great abbey once drew pilgrims here from all over Britain and Europe.

Glastonbury Tor, an odd conical hill with the tower of a ruined church on its summit, can be seen like a beacon from miles around. This, and the nearby ground rising above what used to be an inland sea, was once a sacred island steeped in mystery and legend, the fabled *Ynys Witrin*, or Glassy Isle.

Of Glastonbury's pre-Christian past we know very little. Legends of a holy island of druids and priestesses are hard to prove. Early folk and fairy stories refer to the Tor as an ancient entrance to the underworld. Two springs, one of iron-rich red-coloured water, one white, flow from the two tallest hills and mingle between them.

Did Jesus really visit here? Do King Arthur and Queen Guinevere actually lie buried here in the Avalon of legend? So many of the mysteries surrounding Glastonbury may never be proven.

Today, the ancient abbey is largely ruined and laid low. It has no abbot and is without its monks. But it is still much visited, both by tourists and pilgrims, ordinary and extraordinary people all keen to soak up some of the numinous and magical power of Glastonbury, ancient Isle of Avalon.

THE MENDIPS
secret passages through the landscape

THE MENDIP HILLS run east-west across north Somerset from Frome to Weston-super-Mare on the Bristol Channel. These limestone hills have elevations of about 1000 ft above sea level and are honeycombed with potholes, caves, swallets and underground streams. To the south of the Mendips lie the Somerset levels which were once part of an inland sea that receded leaving a network of rivers, rhines and marshes. In the middle of the levels one can see a distinctive small conical hill – Glastonbury Tor.

Prehistoric man dwelt here. In a cave at Cheddar Gorge Britain's oldest complete skeleton (c. 7000 BC) was found and in caves at Wookey Hole there is evidence of human occupation going back 50,000 years. North of the Mendips are the great stone circles of Stanton Drew dating back to the Bronze Age (c. 2000 BC).

In the peat bogs of the Somerset Levels near Glastonbury the remnants of Iron Age villages have been found along with earlier wooden trackways across the marshes such as the 2500 BC Abbot's Way (*opposite*), linking the islands of Westhay and Burtle, and the Sweet Track (*below*). The latter has been carbon dated to around 3800 BC, a time when basic farming was beginning to replace the initial hunter-gatherer existence of Early Neolithic man.

AN ANCIENT PLANK ROAD CALLED "THE ABBOT'S WAY."

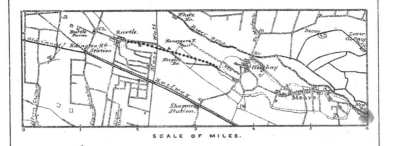

SCALE OF MILES.

Above: The Abbot's Way runs from Burtle to Westhay, both of which were islands standing out from the marshes. The name is a misnomer, since the trackway is carbon-dated to 2500BC, long before there were any abbots living at Glastonbury.

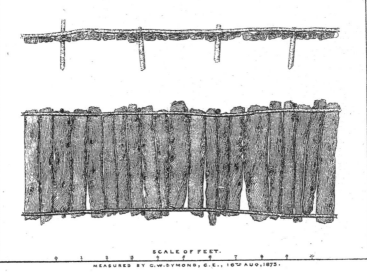

SCALE OF FEET.

MEASURED BY G.W.DYMOND, C.E., 16TH AUG, 1873.

THE ISLE OF AVALON
a secret island

AT THE END OF THE LAST ICE AGE Britain was still joined to what is now France by a land corridor across what is now the English Channel. As the glaciers melted from about 8000 BC the sea level rose rapidly and many coastal areas became inundated. The lowlands of Somerset were turned into an inland sea bordered by salt marshes reaching eastward past Glastonbury.

The only dry land now was the Mendip Hills and the Polden Hills further south. In between, isolated hills, such as Wedmore, Burtle and Meare, stood out of the water as islands. The most distinctive of these was Glastonbury Tor and its surrounding high ground. This was the Isle of Avalon, a secret island surrounded by tidal waters and accessible only by boat or the hidden ancient trackways across marsh and mudflats.

The flooded inland area, later known as the Avalon Marshes, became covered with silt and clay allowing the salt marshes to spread throughout the levels. The rising waters eventually began to recede, and the marshland vegetation over the millennia compacted into layers of peat, up to 20 feet thick, which preserved many wooden and metal artefacts from Neolithic times.

In the 20th century peat-cutters would sometimes discover such hoards. The oldest of the finds were the already mentioned prehistoric wooden trackways, of which more than 43 groups were excavated before their destruction or removal as a result of peat-cutting in the 1970s.

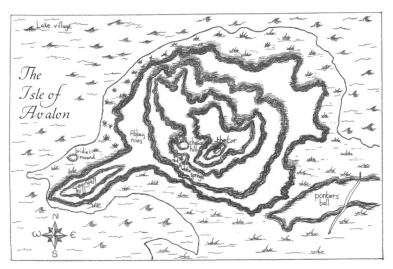

The Isle of Avalon

Lake village

Abbey ruins

bridie's moand

wearyall hill

Chalice hill

thetor

red... springs

ponters ball

N W E S

Above: A map of the Island of Glastonbury, showing the contours and key features: the Tor, Chalice Hill, Chalice Well, Wearyall Hill, Beckery, Lake Village and Ponters Ball. Below: Jane Brayne's drawings of the Glastonbury Lake Village (see next page) in 225BC and 125BC.

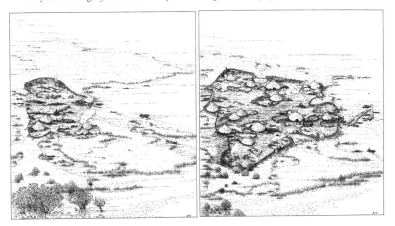

GLASTONBURY LAKE VILLAGE
dwellings in the mists

MARSHLAND SETTLEMENTS thrived in the Avalon Marshes near Glastonbury during the Iron Age (from the 5th to 1st century BC). They are renowned for the remarkable preservation of their timbers, wooden utensils, and woven basketry in the peat bogs. Many of the remains were found by peat cutters but the first major settlement was discovered by Arthur Bulleid in 1892 and named Glastonbury Lake Village. An artificial island built on felled trees with a wooden palisade, it was home to roughly 80 reed-roofed circular huts, each about 18 to 28 ft in diameter with a central hearth and floorboards bedded on clay. It is thought that no more than 14 huts were inhabited at any time from 250 to 50 BC. Finds in the peat have included dugout canoes, ladders, painted pottery (*drawing by Arthur Bulleid below*), bronze bowls, buckets, brooches, saws and chisels.

Living so close to the water in damp and muddy conditions must have led to regular flooding and illnesses which might have been avoided by building on the islands and hills nearby. But such dwellings were secure from enemies and the swamp provided fish, waterbirds and edible plants; and trading boats could moor here too.

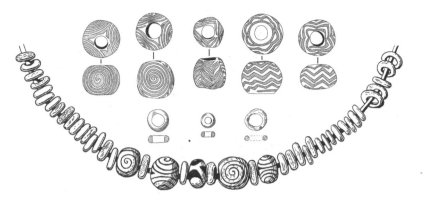

Above: Glass beads found at Meare and a reconstructed necklace (drawing by Mike Rouillard).
Below: A 1911 suggestive painting by A. Forestier of the Glastonbury Lake Village. The village was not created in a lake as the name implies but at the edge of a swamp of reed, sedge and open water between Glastonbury and Godney. There is little to see there now or at other Iron Age marsh settlements that were found near Meare. However, at nearby Westhay, the Peat Moors Visitor Centre has a display of the Lake Village discoveries, a reconstructed Iron Age roundhouse and a wetland walkway.

THE LIE OF THE LAND
the hills and springs

SOMETIMES ONE CAN STAND atop Glastonbury Tor in brilliant sunshine when the surrounding levels are completely hidden under a thick blanket of winter mist. The flat white sea below then resembles the inland sea and marshes which once covered the levels and the high ground appears as islands rising from the mists. To the north one can see the line of the Mendips, under which sits the city of Wells, and to the west the distant Quantocks. The Polden Hills run west–east and curve south as a wooded ridge near Dundon Hill, which is capped with an Iron Age hill-fort.

Three miles east is the ridge of Pennard Hill. In that direction, on a clear day, one can just make out a linear earthwork a mile

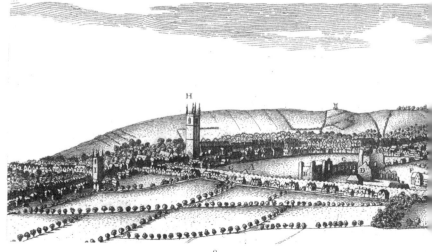

from the Tor called Ponter's Ball. Of Iron Age origin this probably formed some kind of boundary to the sacred Isle of Avalon. The grounds of the ruined Abbey and the town of Glastonbury can be easily seen half a mile to the west, though Chalice Hill, in between, partly obscures the view. Beyond the town rises Wearyall Hill with its special hawthorn tree. 18 miles to the west and north is the coast and the Bristol Channel, from which the island of Steepholm stands clearly. Other prominent landmarks in that direction are Brean Down pointing out to sea and Brent Knoll, a hill with Arthurian connections.

There are many springs around Glastonbury to which we shall return later. In particular, the White Spring issues from the Tor and the legendary Red Spring flows out from Chalice Hill below.

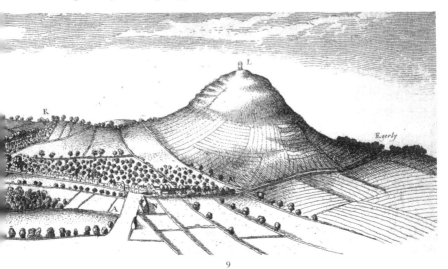

JOSEPH OF ARIMATHEA
and the Holy Thorn

LEGEND HAS IT THAT St Joseph of Arimathea, the uncle of Jesus, made several voyages to England where he traded for tin with miners in Cornwall. On one such trip he brought his young nephew. In turn, Jesus is said to have lived or worked briefly at Priddy, a village seven miles from Glastonbury where there was ancient surface mining. This legend was the basis of William Blake's famous verses 'Jerusalem' with its rhetorical question: *And did those feet in ancient time / Walk upon England's mountains green?*

Years later, after the Crucifixion, in 63 AD St Joseph returned to Somerset as a Christian missionary leading a party of 12 monks from the Holy Land. He paused on Wearyall Hill at Glastonbury where he planted his staff in the ground. It is said to have miraculously burst into leaf showing that it was near here he should settle and build a church. On the hill today a successor winter- and Easter-flowering hawthorn tree is still called the Glastonbury Thorn. Another, in the abbey grounds, supposedly grew from a cutting of the original thorn. A flowering branch from the tree is sent from the abbey each year to decorate the Queen's breakfast table for Christmas Day.

Aviragus, king of this region, granted St Joseph and his followers twelve hides (1440 acres) of land around Glastonbury (*see page 15*) and the very first Christian church in Britain – a circular hut made of wattles like those of the ancient lake villages – was built here in Glastonbury where the present day ruins of the abbey stand.

Above: The Glastonbury Thorn, a Middle Eastern variety, supposedly the living symbol of the first introduction of Christianity into Britain. Below Left: A decorative mount from Meare Village East (drawn by Mike Rouillard). Below Right: The bronze Glastonbury Bowl from Glastonbury Lake Village, Godney. Evidence of fine copper and tin metalwork.

THE OLD CHURCH
first in Britain

THE SMALL ROUND ORATORY built of wattles was held in great veneration, and during the 5th or 6th century a rectangular wooden church was built around it which became known as the Old Church (*vetusta ecclesia*). In about 625 Paulinus, a companion of St Augustine, encased this with lead-covered boards, so that what was left of the old wattle hut was supposedly preserved within.

Such was its sanctity that it drew pilgrims from all over Britain and Ireland and, indeed, the monastic community here was similar in ways to others of the early Celtic church at Clonmacnoise and on Iona. However, Glastonbury was unique in its foundation and dedication. Its first chronicler, William of Malmesbury, was so impressed by the sanctity of the Old Church in 1129 that he wrote of it in awe saying that it spread an air of reverence throughout the whole country. This was the most holy, the most famous and the most revered sanctuary in England, housing many relics and sacred objects which pilgrims could glimpse or touch.

A stone pillar was erected in the 6th century to mark the north-south line delimiting the eastern extent of the Old Church since further building had by then been added to the east.

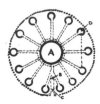

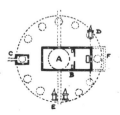

GLASTON·THE·FIRST·CHRISTIAN·SETTLEMENT·A·D·37 WITH WATTLE CHURCH.
COPYRIGHT 1939.

Above: Frederick Bligh Bond's painting of St Joseph's first Christian settlement. Bond envisaged twelve monks' huts arranged around a circular church (see opposite). Circular churches were not unusual in early Christianity. The equally ancient Ethiopian Orthodox Church still has circular churches today.

Above and right: William Barnes' two wood engravings of the Old Church prior to its encasing in lead in 625. Long after the Old Church perished, a brass plaque in Latin was attached to a stone pillar indicating the sacred dimensions of the Old Church and its exact position - vital clues to a sacred foundation pattern to which we shall return later.

13

SEVEN HOLY ISLANDS
and the Saints of Glastonbury

GLASTONBURY'S TWELVE HIDES OF LAND granted to St Joseph were later expanded to include other holy islands where chapels belonging to the abbey stood. Of seven such islands the principal one remained that of Avalon with its Old Church.

A mile west of Glastonbury is Beckery where there was a chapel dedicated to St Brigid who had come to Glastonbury from Kildare in Ireland in the 5th century. Often represented with her cow, a carving of her is found on the ruined church tower on the Tor (*see page 30*). St Patrick, the patron saint of Ireland, is also said to have come here in 433 and to have ended his days as Abbot of Glastonbury. He is said to have been buried in the Old Church and his relics were among the abbey's chief prizes.

St David of Wales arrived at Glastonbury in the 6th century meaning to reconsecrate the Old Church, but did not do so since he had a vision in which he saw that it had already been consecrated by Jesus himself in honour of his mother Mary. His miraculous altar, like a great sapphire, was one of Glastonbury's treasures. Another abbot was St Dunstan who served from 940 to 956 AD. He initiated the construction of many new monastic buildings to the south of the Old Church and under him the abbey's wealth increased until it was among the richest in England.

The relative position of the seven holy islands of Glastonbury is not unlike that of the seven bright stars of the Great Bear (Ursa Major) which is associated with the name of King Arthur.

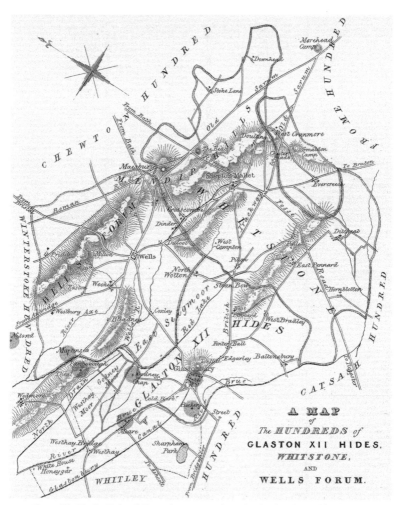

Above: The Twelve Hides of Glastonbury. Apart from the Isle of Avalon itself and Beckery (Bride's Mound), the other five islands close to Glastonbury with chapels were Godney (God's Island), Martinsea (or Marchey), Meare, Panborough and Nyland (Andrewsea).

THE DISASTROUS FIRE OF 1184
and a great discovery

ON MAY 25TH 1184 a terrible fire broke out in the abbey caused by a candle setting light to wall hangings inside. This spread to the Old Church, and other monastic buildings nearby were engulfed in the flames together with many of the holy relics. All of these were burned to ashes. It seemed like a blow from which the abbey could never recover and the number of pilgrims soon dwindled.

Within two years the Chapel of St Mary which we see today had been built precisely on the site where the Old Church had once stood. This remarkable church with its two Romanesque doorways in the north and the south walls would eventually become the west end of the great abbey itself that rose phoenix-like from the ashes of its predecessor. Even today this, of all parts of the ruined abbey, seems to resonate with the pure energy of the sanctity of the Old Church.

However, well before much of this new abbey was built, the monks, while digging in the ancient burial ground to the south of the St Mary Chapel in 1191, made a quite extraordinary discovery. They found a double oak coffin buried 16 ft below the ground and containing the bones of a tall man and a woman whose long golden hair was still preserved. We will consider whose bones these were.

THE ST MARY CHAPEL
and its geometry

THE BASIS OF GLASTONBURY'S foundation pattern was recorded in Latin on a 14th century brass plaque (now lost). It told of the coming of Joseph of Arimathea and his followers "in the 31st year after the Passion of our Lord". Also of the dedication by Christ of the original church that stood here to his mother. It gave the dimensions of the Old Church as 60 ft by 26ft. The pillar on which the plaque was fixed was erected by St David 48 ft from the midpoint of its east wall and showed its easternmost extent.

In 1918 Bligh Bond wrote of specific messages from mediums relating to Glastonbury's foundation pattern. These told of a floor pattern in the Old Church with a central hub surrounded by the twelve zodiacal signs. These corresponded to the twelve apostles and the twelve hermit cells of St Joseph. Bond interpreted this with a diagram of a hexagon enclosing the Mary Chapel (*below left*).

A more satisfactory solution is offered by John Michell who has proposed an octagonal foundation pattern (*below right*) based on the dimensions of the Old Church and the existing Mary Chapel.

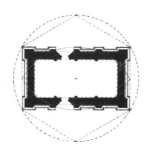
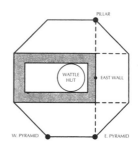

Above: The ruins of the Mary Chapel. Right: 16th century illustration from Spelman's Concilia of the brass plaque once found on St. David's Pillar. Opposite: Bligh Bond's hexagonal pattern and John Michell's octagonal pattern. The octagon is fixed by the two west corners of the Mary chapel. One of its two parallel north-south chords passes through the middle of the north and south doors of the chapel and terminates on Bligh Bond's (west) "pyramid." The other coincides with the east wall of the chapel terminating at one end on St David's pillar and at the other end on the suggested position of the east pyramid. At the centre of the octagon lies the original circular wattle church. This pattern can also be proportionately related to the layout of Stonehenge, built nearly three and half millennia earlier.

Anno post passione domini xxxi duodem sci et quibz uenerut qui ecciam huic regni prima in hoc loco construerut qui hijc i honor sue mris a loci pcoru sepultura psencialit dedicaunt sco dauid meneuecu archiebo hic restrauit Qui dns ecciam illa dedicari te disponeci in sopnis apparuit a eu a proposito resio caut nemo i signu qd ipe dns ecciam ipam prius cu cimiterio dedicarat manu epi digito pforauit a sic i forata multis uidentibz i crastino apparuit postea uo ide epc dno reuelate ac scro humo in eade crelcebit queda cancellu i orientali parte huic ecce adiecit a honorc beate uirginis ueneraut quaaltare lestimabili saphiro i petua hui rei memoria signiunt Et ne loc aut quntitas ipsius ecce p tales anguteracoes obliuioni traderet erigitur

sic columna linea p duos orientales angulos eiusdc ecce ipso indiem p tracta p pucti carcelli ab ea abscisa cente et erat et logitudo ab illa linea ipso euidente lx pedu latitudo uo ee xxvi pedu distancia centri istic columpne a puncto medio re pdictos angulos xlviii pedum

KING ARTHUR'S TOMB
the holy grail of royal relics

THE MONKS IN 1191 HAD FIRST UNCOVERED a thick stone slab above the coffin and there, attached to its underside, they found a "leaden" cross bearing the inscription "*Hic iacet sepultus inclitus Rex Arturius in insula Avalonia*". This translates as "Here lies buried the famous King Arthur in the Isle of Avalon".

Obviously these were the mortal remains of King Arthur and his Queen, Guinevere. This was a major discovery, and seemed to confirm without a shred of doubt the legend that Glastonbury was, indeed, the mythical realm of Avalon.

Modern day historians, however, are largely sceptical of this whole story, claiming that it was probably contrived by the monks with a view to restoring the fortunes of the abbey after the devastation of the fire. That must have been to some extent the case, but if there really was an historical King Arthur who ruled in these parts in about 450 AD, then Glastonbury Abbey would indeed have been the logical place to bury him. The ground near the Old Church was the holiest in England and most fit for an illustrious king. After all, it had long been held to be the final resting place of Joseph of Arimathea.

The remains were preserved as relics in the St Mary Chapel and in 1278, in the presence of Edward I, they were ceremonially re-interred in a fine black marble tomb in the newly built abbey church. There they remained until the dissolution in 1539. The tomb's position is still marked today.

Above: The remaining two pillars of the central crossing, just
east of which lay the site of the of the tomb of Arthur and Guinevere. Right: The lead cross bearing the inscription about Arthur.
It passed into private hands at the dissolution and was lost.
There have been reports of its brief reappearance, most recently
in 1981, but none can be confirmed as being of the original cross.
Like other Arthurian legends this too is a mystery. Below: An
ancient altar tomb from St John's church in Glastonbury.

ARTHURIAN LEGEND
and the quest for the holy grail

FROM THOSE EARLY TIMES the Legend of King Arthur and his Knights of the Round Table has developed and grown like that of no other national hero. Volumes of literature have been written about Arthur and Camelot and the Quest for the Holy Grail – not just in England but many other countries. Certainly the vast bulk of this great corpus of Arthurian legend is romanticised fiction, but it is quite probable that this was based on an historic tribal leader. The name Arthur is from the Welsh term for "great bear".

Camelot is thought to have been the prominent Iron Age hill-fort Cadbury Castle which lies 11 miles to the south-east of Glastonbury. According to legend, this was the site of King Arthur's palace and his Round Table. The Holy Grail, favourite subject of Arthurian quest, was supposedly the chalice used at the Last Supper and to catch the blood of Christ when he was speared upon the cross. St Joseph of Arimathea is said to have brought this vessel, which had miraculous powers, to Glastonbury and it was buried by him under Chalice Hill between the abbey and the Tor.

The quest for the Grail is ultimately the journey of the seeker-after-truth, and the importance of spiritual purity in such pursuits is emphasised again and again in the later Arthurian literature.

Left: A replica of Arthur's Round Table (from the Great Hall in Winchester).

Below and opposite: Cadbury Castle, supposed site of Camelot. The quest for the Grail was first described by Chrétien de Troyes. He tells the story of Sir Perceval, one of Arthur's knights, who sees the Grail carried in a procession at the palace of the Fisher King. Only the simple Perceval and the saintly Sir Galahad can look on the Grail, shining with the divine light, without discomfort. In Old French "graal", or "san greal", means "Holy Grail" while "sang real" means "royal blood"; later writers played on this pun.

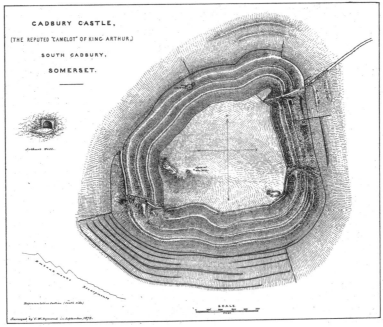

CADBURY CASTLE,

(THE REPUTED "CAMELOT" OF KING ARTHUR,)

SOUTH CADBURY,

SOMERSET.

Arthur's Well.

SCALE

Surveyed by C.W. Dymond in September, 1875.

THE GREAT ABBEY
longest in Britain

DURING THE 13TH CENTURY, construction of the great abbey church continued until its completion in 1278 when Arthur and Guinevere were re-interred there. Its cruciform shape extended a vast 580 feet from the western end of the St Mary Chapel to its eastern end, an area larger than Canterbury Cathedral. A huge square bell tower stood at the crossing. In the same period a large cloister, and many other monastic buildings, such as the refectory (monk's dining hall), and a dorter (monk's dormitory) were added. The west front was built with twin flanking towers soon after 1250 and for many years the furnishing and decoration of the church went on, with vaulting of the nave and extensive painting continuing well into the 14th century.

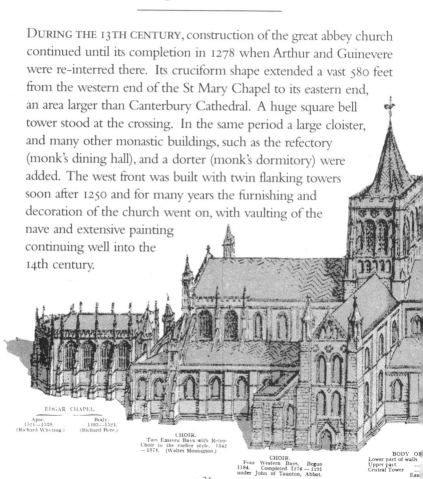

EDGAR CHAPEL.

Apse.
1521—1539.
(Richard Whyting.)

Body.
1193—1524.
(Richard Bere.)

CHOIR.
Two Eastern Bays with Retro-
Choir in the earlier style. 1342
—1374. (Walter Monington.)

CHOIR.
Four Western Bays, Begun
1184. Completed 1274 — 1291
under John of Taunton, Abbot.

BODY O
Lower part of walls
Upper part
Central Tower
Eas

In the early 14th century the Mary Chapel, which had stood alone, was joined by a processional building, known as the Galilee, to the west entrance of the abbey church. In about 1500, Abbot Richard Beere built the crypt under the Mary Chapel (still seen today), dedicating it to St Joseph. In doing so, he excavated the holy ground on which the original wattle church of St Joseph had stood. On the east end of the abbey Beere built the Edgar Chapel, designed to house memorials to the Saxon King Edgar, held to have been one of the abbey's great benefactors. The foundations of this were later to be excavated by Bligh Bond.

Left: The abbey as it looked shortly before its destruction in 1539. A detailed model can be found in the abbey museum.

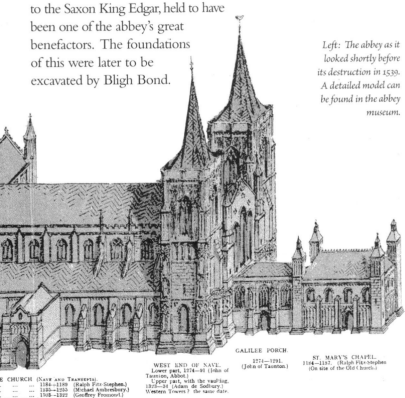

E CHURCH (NAVE AND TRANSEPTS).
.. .. 1184—1189 (Ralph Fitz-Stephen.)
.. .. 1235—1255 (Michael Ambresbury.)
.. .. 1303—1322 (Geoffrey Fromond.)
of Nave vaulted by the same Abbot.

WEST END OF NAVE.
Lower part, 1274—91 (John of Taunton, Abbot.)
Upper part, with the vaulting, 1323—34 (Adam de Sodbury.)
Western Towers ? the same date.

GALILEE PORCH.
1274—1291.
(John of Taunton.)

ST. MARY'S CHAPEL.
1184—1187. (Ralph Fitz-Stephen on site of the Old Church.)

THE POWER OF THE ABBOT
and his mighty kitchen

In the 10th century, under Abbot Dunstan, the abbey was re-established under the Benedictine Order and began to receive the official patronage of the crown. By 1086, at the time of the Domesday Book, Glastonbury was the richest monastery in Britain.

The monks spent much of their time in prayer, services and, under St Benedicts spartan regime, ate and drank very little. In contrast, the abbot (not bound by dietary rules) had his own dining hall, separate from the monks, and, nearby, his own splendid Kitchen where great feasts were prepared for him and his guests, such as Henry VII and Henry VIII. With its high octagonal pyramid and tower over a square base, this is one of the few abbey buildings that remain intact today.

The wealth and the power of the great abbey and its considerable land holdings in Somerset increased until the 16th century by which time it had become a major political force.

Left and below: The 14th century Abbot's Kitchen. In its interior corners four huge fireplaces heated ovens in the walls and cauldrons full of food. Abbey records show that huge quantities of meat, fish, bread and wine were regularly prepared here. Just the southwest angle of the abbot's great dining hall remains standing today, and the abbot's house, as fine as any bishop's palace, remained intact well into the 18th century when it was demolished. By 1500 Glastonbury was the second wealthiest abbey in Britain, after Westminster, and the abbot lived in great state.

Opposite: The great Abbey Tithe Barn, on the corner of Chilkwell Street, now site of the Somerset Rural Life Museum.

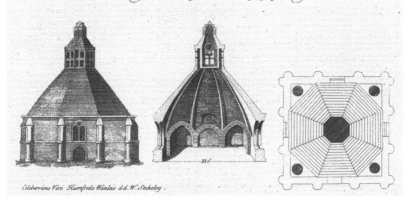

The Orthography Section, & Groundplot of the Abbot of Glasenburys Kitchin. Aug. 17. 1723.

33 f.

Celeberrimo Viro Humfredo Wanleio d.d. W. Stukeley.

GLASTONBURY TOR
at the centre of the world

A ROUNDED HILL shaped somewhat like a female breast, rising above the east side of the town not far beyond the abbey, Glastonbury Tor consists of layered clay and blue lias stone with a cap of hard Midford sandstone. From its 520 ft summit there are magnificent views across the Somerset levels surrounding it of the Bristol Channel to the west and the Mendip Hills to the north. Scattered finds of prehistoric, Roman and later objects suggest it has long been used by man. Indications of Christian monks' cells from 900–1100 AD have been found cut in the rock on the summit.

Some believe that the sculptured terraces which wind around the slopes of the Tor were built by the monks as a processional pathway to the summit. Others think the terraced slopes constituted a much earlier mystical maze or labyrinth (*below, from Russell Scott & Geoffrey Ashe*). It has been suggested that such an ancient pagan ritual pathway was connected with worship of the Earth Mother goddess. A more conventional view is that the terraces were made by the monks for the purpose of growing produce or planting vines.

When there was a 19th century resurgence of interest in Celtic Mythology, the Tor became associated with Gwyn ap Nudd who was first Lord of the Underworld, and later King of the Fairies.

Above and below: Views of Glastonbury Tor. After the 19th century Celtic renaissance the Tor was often described as an entrance to the underworld or realm of the fairies. A supposedly earlier myth was that St Collen, a hermit and an early Abbot of Glastonbury, once climbed to the top of the Tor by hacking his way through thick undergrowth. Once there he found a great gathering of the fairy folk who were feasting and making music. They invited him to join them but in alarm the monk took out a flask of holy water and sprinkled it over them causing them to disappear and leaving him alone on the hilltop. Today the Tor is managed by the National Trust who have spent considerable money repairing and stabilising the tower of St Michael's church on the summit.

ST MICHAEL'S ON THE TOR
all that remains

THE ROOFLESS CHURCH TOWER which stands on the Tor today dates from the 14th century and was part of the second of two major churches which occupied the summit. Dedicated to St Michael, this church was closely associated with the abbey and was probably built 50 years after the earthquake of 1275 which destroyed its predecessor. After the dissolution of the monasteries in 1539 the church fell into ruin and the tower is all that is left.

The Archangel Michael was often associated with high places and poorly defined carving of him trampling a dragon is still discernible on the southwest face of the tower. The tower and church were aligned nearly 30 degrees off the normal east–west axis due principally to the fact that the backbone of the Tor's summit, and the Michael Line (*next page*), runs in this direction.

An ancient prophecy stated that "*When a fysshe upon ye Torr is caught, then shall ye Abbey comme to naught*". We shall see later the grotesque way in which this prophecy was fulfilled.

Above: The tower of the ruined St Michael's church on the Tor. Left: Somewhat fanciful wood engravings by William Barnes of the carvings on the tower. To the left we see St Michael weighing souls. To the right St Brigid is seen milking her cow.

THE ST MICHAEL LINE
a caduceus across the land

DURING THE 1960S AND 70S John Michell published his research on a remarkable alignment of sacred sites along what he called the St Michael line. This straight alignment crosses southern England from a point near Land's End in Cornwall to the eastern coast of Suffolk passing through or close to several major sanctuaries dedicated to St Michael such as the church on Glastonbury Tor, and those at Burrowbridge, Brentor, Roche Rock and St Michael's Mount. Besides these, the alignment goes through other ancient sites like Avebury Henge, the Cheesewring rock formation in Cornwall, Carn Brea, St George's Church in Ogbourne St George, Royston Cave and Bury St Edmunds Abbey. It is the longest line across land that can be drawn through southern England and its eastern part coincides with the ancient track known as the Icknield Way.

More than 20 sites, both natural and human made, lie exactly on or close to this line – hardly the result of mere chance. It seems the ancients were aware of the St Michael line and that some artificial sites such as Avebury were intentionally built on it.

In 1990 Hamish Miller and Paul Broadhurst published *The Sun and the Serpent*. This tells how Miller, starting in Cornwall, had dowsed near the alignment and detected a strong current of earth energy which wound on either side of it. This "male" energy he called the St Michael current. They traced it across St Michael's Mount and other sacred sites towards Glastonbury. Later a "female" St Mary current was discovered, winding similarly across the country.

Above: St Michael's church on Burrow Mump resembles a baby Tor exactly on the St Michael alignment. Below: the St Michael Line across southeren England. On either side of it wind the serpent-like Michael and Mary currents of telluric energies dowsed and plotted by Miller and Broadhurst.

THE FALL OF THE ABBEY
the great divorce

BY THE START OF THE 16TH CENTURY Glastonbury Abbey had become a power to be reckoned with and among the wealthiest of Britain's 800 monasteries. When, in 1529, Henry VIII wanted to divorce his first wife, Catherine of Aragon so that he could marry Anne Boleyn, his petition was denied by the Pope. Three years later a new Archbishop of Canterbury, Cranmer, declared Henry's marriage to Catherine invalid and Anne was quickly crowned queen.

This led to excommunication by the Pope. In response the Act of Supremacy was passed by Parliament, declaring Henry supreme head of a new Church of England, breaking with Rome. Most of the abbots and monks, including Richard Whiting, the incumbent Abbot of Glastonbury, took the oath to the King upholding the new Act.

But Henry did not stop there. During the next seven years over 10,000 monks and nuns were driven out of their monasteries and the buildings seized by the Crown to fill Henry's depleted coffers. Among the last to suffer this enforced dissolution was Glastonbury.

The fate of Richard Whiting was particularly savage. In 1539 he was arrested and found guilty of various trumped up charges, such as stealing and concealing the abbey's treasures. He was sentenced to be hung, drawn and quartered. On November 15th he was dragged up the Tor bound to a hurdle, and executed beside St Michael's Church with two of his monks. Later he was cut down and dismembered, his head being stuck on a pike and displayed at the abbey gateway and his limbs exhibited in Bath, Wells, Ilchester and Bridgwater.

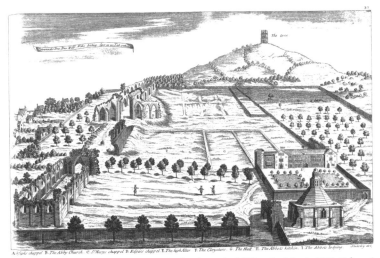

A. St Joseph chappel B. The Abby Church C. S.t Maryes chappel D. Edgars chappel E. The high Alter F. The Cloysters G. The Hall H. The Abbots kitchin I. The Abbots lodging Stukeley del.

Above: "The Prospect of Glastonbury Abbey" as drawn by William Stukeley in 1723. Below: A view of the Joseph Chapel, looking east, from Frederick Ross's 1882 book "Ruined Abbeys".

DISPERSAL AND DECAY
the loss of the library

THUS THE OLD PROPHECY was fulfilled with the wretched Whiting (a most unexpected fish) being 'caught' upon the Tor. The great abbey of Glastonbury was doomed. The other 40 monks were driven out of the abbey and whatever treasures could be found were confiscated and sold off. The deeds of its extensive land holdings were gathered by agents of the Crown and appropriated by the King.

One of the greatest losses was that of the Glastonbury library, which had housed rare ancient histories of England and many unique early Christian documents like illuminated manuscripts which must have equalled such treasures as the Book of Kells. There were alchemical texts and books of learning that could never be replaced. When Henry VIII's librarian John Leland first saw these literary treasures he fainted with wonder, but the library was looted and dispersed and priceless manuscripts used in local shops as wrapping paper. It is, however, likely that the most prized treasures were concealed by the monks on the orders of Abbot Whiting before he was arrested and hanged. Even under torture he never revealed their whereabouts.

The abbey was left closed and empty following the dissolution of 1539. But soon the people of Glastonbury and the surrounding country were helping themselves to whatever remained. It became a quarry with stone being plundered and used to build or repair houses in the town. Much went into construction of the new causeway road to Wells. Carts removed the best building stone, and for 300 years stone moved from the abbey into the town.

Above: The old market cross, with the Bacchus-like figure of Jack Stagg on top.
Below: Another view of the ruined abbey.

GLASTONBURY TOWN
the husk around the ruined abbey

AT THE CENTRE OF GLASTONBURY TOWN is the ruined Abbey enclosed in a square by four roads, each of about a quarter mile's length. On the north side is the busy High Street, containing a 15th century hostelry, now the George and Pilgrims Hotel, built by Abbot Selwood for pilgrims to the Abbey. Not far from this is the Tribunal (*lower opposite*), and further up the street is St John's Church (C of E) with its stained glass window depicting Joseph of Arimathea.

In Magdalene Street, west of the Abbey, is St Mary's Church (RC) containing a tapestry commemorating the old saints of Glastonbury and martyrs Abbot Whiting and his two fellow monks who were executed on the Tor. There is a statue of Our Lady of Glastonbury.

Many shops in the High Street and Magdalene Street today are devoted to esoteric and mystical merchandise. But to many people Glastonbury is best known for its famous pop music festival, held at Pilton, five miles away.

Above: An early view up the High Street showing the George and Pilgrims Hotel on the left.

Left: The Tribunal, built by Abbot Beere c. 1500, was the Court House for the Twelve Hides of Glastonbury and is now the Tourist Information Centre and Lake Village Museum.

Opposite: Although it was yet another adjunct of the Abbey, the Great Tithe Barn in Bere Lane is no longer part of it and has become the Somerset Rural Life Museum which illustrates the tools and techniques of farming during the Victorian era. It also describes unusual local activities like willow growing, mud horse fishing, peat digging and cider making.

WELLS CATHEDRAL
built on springs

THE BUILDING OF A CHURCH beside the great spring at Wells, five miles northeast of Glastonbury took place about 705 AD during the reign of King Ine of Wessex. This church was extended and rebuilt until work began on a cathedral in 1176. A magnificent Gothic edifice with high pointed arches and clustered columns, Wells Cathedral was similar in many respects to the Abbey of Glastonbury, only it survived whereas Glastonbury did not.

The west front has the largest array of mediaeval sculpture surving from the 12th and 13th centuries in Britain, consisting mostly of saints, kings and ecclesiastics. The great scissor arches which support the cathedral's central tower are similar to those once present at Glastonbury Abbey. The octagonal chapter house with its central pillar and fan tracery is particularly fine. There is also a moated Bishop's Palace and a street of mediaeval houses, known as Vicar's Close, dating from about 1350.

The cathedral has a mediaeval clock made in about 1390. The outer circle of its dial has the 24 hours marked round it and a pointer tipped with the sun shows the current hour. Inside this another concentric circle has minutes which are indicated by a smaller sun pointer. Within that an inner circle shows the age and phase of the moon. On a platform above the clock, model knights on horseback joust on contra-rotating mechanisms whenever the quarter hour strikes. The same knight is always struck down by his victorious opponent coming round in the opposite direction.

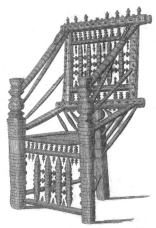

Above left: The Wells Cathedral clock is a representation of the mediaeval universe with earth at the centre and the sun going round it, highest at noon at the top of the clock and lowest at midnight. Above the earth are the stars and in the corners of the heavens angels are to be found. Above right: Abbot Whiting's chair, now in Wells. Below: An 1850's view of the Cathedral.

SPRINGS AND HOLY WELLS
an island of many waters

ONE OF THE LEGENDS OF GLASTONBURY is that Joseph of Arimathea buried the Holy Grail under Chalice Hill, causing the Red, or Blood, Spring to flow out of the hill. The water runs through the Grail and is stained red by the blood of Christ, which Joseph caught in the chalice when Christ was nailed to the cross. This spring, or well, is in the Chalice Well Gardens off Chilkwell Street, the street name being a corruption of "chalice well". However, this "chalice" might equally be a corruption of "chalybeate" which is the term used for such reddish-brown spring water rich in iron.

Another version is that the Red Spring of the Chalice Well and the White Spring, which flows from under the Tor, come from the two flasks, one bearing Christ's blood and the other his sweat, which St Joseph brought to Glastonbury. This rather conflicts with the general belief that Joseph was buried, together with the two flasks, in the grounds of the Abbey just south of the Mary Chapel. In the crypt here, called the Joseph Chapel, is a further holy well, St Joseph's Well, which was clearly a place of importance to pilgrims in the early days of the Abbey.

The White Spring once flowed from the foot of the Tor into the small valley beside the chalice well. Its well was destroyed when a reservoir building to catch its waters replaced it in 1872. A number of other abandoned springs and ruined holy wells surround Glastonbury. St Edmund's spring is now a modern goldfish pond, Paradise Well, near the Gog & Magog oaks, is a sealed brick trough.

Above left: A holy well in Glastonbury. *Above right:* A view of the entrace into the pentagonal chamber within the Chalice Well. *Below:* St Joseph's Well in the crypt of the Mary Chapel. The crypt was dedicated to St Joseph of Arimathea in about 1500.

BLIGH BOND'S EXCAVATIONS
and the spiritual renaissance

IN THE FIRST YEARS OF THE 20th century the Church of England bought the abbey ruins at auction and began excavations there. From 1909 these were directed by Frederick Bligh Bond who made several remarkable finds including the base of a pillar marking the eastern limit of the Old Church, and a pyramid-shaped monument which had stood directly out from the south door of the St Mary chapel. He believed this was one of two such monuments marking the position of Arthur's grave and that the pillar and these markers were significant points of Glastonbury's Foundation Pattern.

The church authorities became alarmed when they heard of the interest in Bond's finds and the way in which he had supposedly been led to them. Being of a mystical disposition he had sought contact with the spirits of dead monks through mediums and by the use of automatic writing (*below*). The apparent success of this spirit guidance encouraged him and his followers to believe they were on the verge of a major discovery – perhaps even the Holy Grail itself.

In 1922 Bond was dismissed from his position and the church authorities permanently excluded him from the Abbey grounds.

44

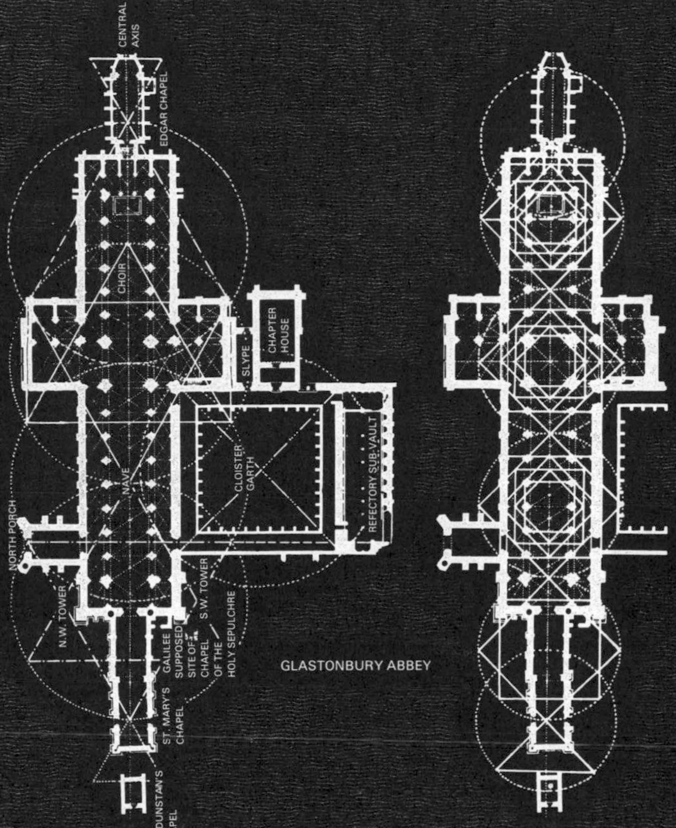
CENTRAL AXIS
EDGAR CHAPEL
CHOIR
CHAPTER HOUSE
SLYPE
CLOISTER GARTH
REFECTORY SUB-VAULT
NAVE
NORTH PORCH
N.W. TOWER
S.W. TOWER
GALILEE
SUPPOSED SITE OF CHAPEL OF THE HOLY SEPULCHRE
ST. MARY'S CHAPEL
ST. DUNSTAN'S CHAPEL
GLASTONBURY ABBEY

The Ad Triangulum (left) and Ad Quatratum (right) systems of integrated geometry which underlie the plan of Glastonbury Abbey (after Nigel Pennick).

CHALICE WELL & GARDENS
the red spring and the white spring

THE ABUNDANT RED SPRING, delivering 25,000 gallons of water a day, flows out from under Chalice Hill and down through the Chalice Well gardens. These are owned and managed by a Trust, founded by Glastonbury mystic Wellesley Tudor Pole in 1959. The red-coloured chalybeate spring, which has never failed, is considered an ancient holy well and its waters are said to have healing properties. One may drink this spring water in the gardens where they flow out from the Lion's Head spout, or in Wellhouse Lane, outside, where the water pours from the wall. Opposite, across the road, the clear waters of the White Spring flow from under the Tor (*drawing of the Tor below by Nicholas Mann*).

The Chalice Well is often portrayed as a symbol of the female aspect of deity, with the male aspect symbolised by the nearby Tor and White Spring. The Well is popular with all faiths and was designated a World Peace Garden in 2001.

Left: The well-head of the Red Spring has an oak and wrought iron cover in the form of a Vesica Piscis, the symbol associated with Glastonbury by Bligh Bond. Lower down in 'King Arthur's Courtyard,' through which the stream flows, the Vesica symbol is crossed by a sword representing King Arthur's Excalibur. In the lowest part of the gardens the rusty waters pour through vulvic cascades into a pool, once again shaped like the Vesica Piscis. Drawing by Christina Martin.

Below: Another watery connection: The opening of the wool traders' Glastonbury canal in 1833.

ASTRONOMY AND GEOMETRY
great order in the landscape

THE TWELVE HIDES and the seven holy islands of Glastonbury formed the basis of a pattern that reflected the perfection of the heavens above. The seven islands corresponded to the stars of the Great Bear with the Tor as the Pole Star, a theme repeated in the floor pattern of the Old Church with the twelve signs of the Zodiac around the centre of the circle, and the twelve monastic cells of his followers around St Joseph's old wattle oratory.

This mystical idea of recreating heaven on earth by the use of geometry and sacred number is very ancient and is found in the designs of many sacred sites including Stonehenge and the Gizeh pyramids. It was therefore tempting for Katherine Maltwood to claim in 1935 that the landscape around Glastonbury was fashioned into the outlines of the various creatures of the Zodiac such as Leo, Taurus, Capricorn, and Virgo. For some this was the discovery of a holy grail although others found it unconvincing.

More relevant to the Glastonbury mystery is the simple symbol of the vesica piscis. This consists of two equal overlapping circles, with the centre of one on the circumference of the other. The Latin words mean literally "bladder of the fish" and the central almond-shaped part of the design was an early Christian symbol for Christ.

Shown below and opposite are various strange marriages of geometry, landscape and architecture around Glastonbury.

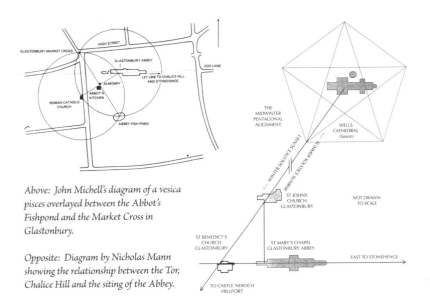

Above: John Michell's diagram of a vesica pisces overlayed between the Abbot's Fishpond and the Market Cross in Glastonbury.

Opposite: Diagram by Nicholas Mann showing the relationship between the Tor, Chalice Hill and the siting of the Abbey.

Above right: Kenneth Knight's discovery of the pentagonally based midsummer-midwinter alignment from Glastonbury to Wells Cathedral. Also shows the easterly Stonehenge alignment.

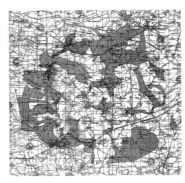

Above: Katherine Maltwood's landscape zodiac of fields centred on Butleigh woods.

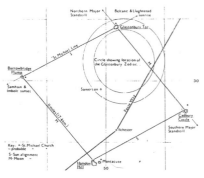

Above: A lunar extreme and cross-quarter parallelogram of major iron-age hillforts in the area

A SACRED CENTRE
still a place of pilgrimage

TODAY IN THE EARLY YEARS of the new millennium, Glastonbury is still a sacred centre, a place of pilgrimage, and visitors are drawn here for a variety of reasons, often hard to define.

Numerous gatherings and conferences occur in the town every year with spiritual or esoteric themes, covering subjects as diverse as megaliths, crop circles, Buddhism, UFOs, sacred geometry, yoga, earth energies, Celtic Christianity, and metrology. There are gatherings of druids, pagans, goddess worshippers, holistic healers and a major Christian pilgrimage to the town and abbey every summer. Finally, of course, there is the famous Glastonbury Festival held in nearby Pilton. Evidently the name of Glastonbury still holds a mystique which draws people from all over the world.

How much of Glastonbury's story is fact and how much is fiction? Did Joseph of Arimathea really come here from the Holy Land and establish the very first Christian church in this place? Was Glastonbury King Arthur's Avalon? Was it really Arthur and Guinevere that the monks dug up in the abbey in 1191? Is the St Michael alignment proof that the ancients knew of ley lines and their associated telluric energies spanning England?

The truth or otherwise of all these ancient mysteries is something that each of us should decide. It is not something that one will necessarily find in the pages of this book or any other. It is best to come to Glastonbury, to linger a while, and let the magic of this ancient place speak to you itself.

GLASTONBURY WALK I - 1.5 MILES
Over Glastonbury Tor and Back

From the Market Cross in the centre of town, walk all the way up the High Street, turn right at the top and after a few minutes left into Dod Lane. Where the lane curves left, go straight ahead taking the path uphill due east towards the Tor. This joins a road briefly but continue straight, and go across a field to reach the road that goes around the base of the Tor. Go left on this briefly and then turn right into the field where a concrete path leads one, in about 10 minutes, to the summit of the Tor.

One can inspect the ruined tower of St Michael's

Church here and take in the breathtaking views of the surrounding countryside. Then go down the Tor by the path on the other side of the summit. This leads southwest down into Wellhouse Lane coming out opposite Chalice Well Gardens.

Turn right at the main road (Chilkwell Street, here part of the A361) and walk to the mini-roundabout. Take the left hand branch of the road (Bere Lane, still A361) past the Abbey Tithe Barn until one gets to Magdalene Street at the end. Turn right into this and follow back to the Market Cross.

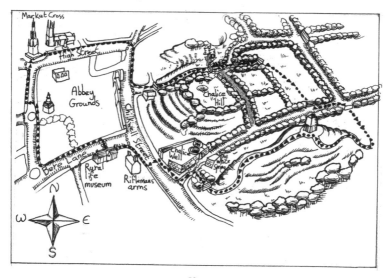

GLASTONBURY WALK II - A MILE
From the Tor to Gog and Magog Oaks

At the bottom of the north way up the Tor (just described in Walk I) there is a bus stop, but parking here is permanently prohibited. From here walk half a mile east on a lane going down hill. Turn left at the bottom and after a few minutes one reaches the ancient oak trees known as Gog and Magog, supposedly the only survivors of a sacred druidic grove. Turn left into the field opposite the oaks and head back up hill following the footpath. The track swings round to the right along the upper rim of a valley leading into a short lane going west. Where this meets the road turn left and follow the road back to the bus stop below the Tor.

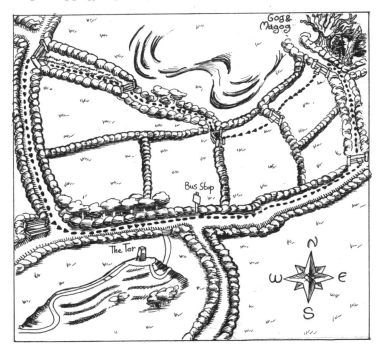

GLASTONBURY WALK III - ½ MILE
Round Glastonbury Abbey Grounds

One must pay an entrance fee to go round the Abbey but one can take as long as one likes during opening hours. Enter from Magdalene Street and start this self-guided tour from the chapel dedicated to St Patrick near the entrance. Beyond this is a hawthorn tree said to be from a cutting of St Joseph's Holy Thorn. A little beyond are the fine ruins of the St Mary Chapel built on the site of the original Old Church. Visit its crypt and holy well. Then walk out on the south side to the spot where the monks exhumed King Arthur in 1191. From here we walk east through the ruins of the great Abbey Church. At the crossing of the transepts and the choir one finds the site of the tomb where King Arthur was reinterred. A little beyond is where the High Altar stood. At the extreme east end are the remains of the Edgar Chapel from which one can see the alignment of the distant St Benedict's church with the centre line of the Abbey Church. Next, walk to and around the pond in the eastern part of the grounds. From there one can walk to the western elliptical Abbot's Fishpond, full of water lilies, which lies 250 yds south of the Abbey. Going back toward the ruined cloisters and other levelled stonework one passes an herb garden. Then go west to the conical-shaped Abbot's Kitchen which has interesting displays within. Finally back to the visitor centre where there is a fascinating museum containing among other things a model of the abbey before its destruction.

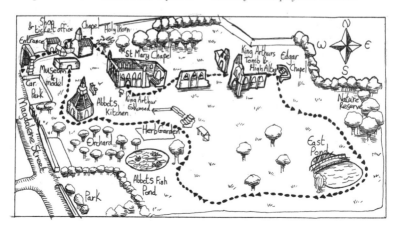

GLASTONBURY WALK IV - 2 MILES
Wearyall Hill and Bride's Mound

Start from a pull-in beside Roman Way towards the top of Wearyall Hill. Enter the field and take footpath up hill to the Glastonbury Thorn. From here one has a panoramic view of the town, the Tor and the levels. Continue west along ridge of hill and then left down into the Roman Way again. This leads to the main road (A361) where it crosses the River Brue at Pomparles Bridge. Go over pedestrian crossing and enter field on the north side of the Brue. Cross field towards a mobile phone transmitter mast, leaving Bridie's Yard (a hippie encampment) to the right. Come out on a road. It goes right; you continue on and turn left through a gate into a long field. Walk up the field going away from the phone mast. Bride's Mound,

where St Brigid lived and where there was once a chapel, is the elevated ground at the top of the field. There is a sewage works to the right. Go back towards the mast and take the road east briefly, before turning right towards the A361. Cross A361 here to a small war memorial, and then over stile to footpath east along side of a rhine. Walk 600 yds to weir where this meets the River Brue. Cross left over rhine by bridge near Clyse Hole sluice. Go right over further bridge and then walk in direction of the east end of Wearyall Hill. Turn left on a footpath up hill which goes back into Roman Way. Turn right, and then left at mini-roundabout, still on Roman Way. This shortly brings you back to where you started.

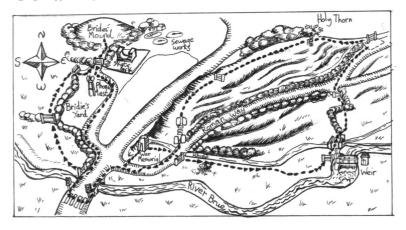

GLASTONBURY WALK V - 6 MILES
Walton Hill & Compton Dundon via Hood Monument

This long circular walk can be shortened by omitting the final part (after Compton Dundon), thus making it a one-way walk. Start from the small NT car park on Walton Hill. Walk SE on path to hilltop with orientation table and pointer to the Hood Monument. Take footpath through woods in this direction, first S of the road, then across (along past YHA building) until reaching crossroads. Cross over and continue SE over Collard Hill (NT), through three kissing gates into the woods and across a minor road to Hood Monument, a 110 ft obelisk to Admiral Sir Samuel Hood (d. 1814). Go S from obelisk down a steep path onto the minor road and follow this down to the village of Compton Dundon, walking Compton Street to the main road (B3151). Left here 200 yds to the Castlebrook Inn, a pleasant pub with all-day opening. This is halfway.

Exit the inn and turn right (along B3151). First left (Ham Lane) for 300 yds then second footpath on left which leads SW towards Compton Dundon Church.

Follow path with paving stones obliquely across field through a farmyard into School Lane. Up to the left is thickly-wooded Dundon Hill, a splendid Iron Age hill-fort (visit if time). Rejoin road briefly and then turn sharp left up to St Andrew's Church in Dundon with its massive yew tree thought to be 1,000 years old. From the church, go N on the road about 250 yds, then straight ahead on Hurst Drove which ends but footpath continues N toward Ivy Thorn Manor. The path along the hedge goes briefly right into another field, then N again, left out of it, and N again until reaching a minor lane. Go W toward Middle Ivy Thorn Farm. Keep on track W, although lane turns SW.

Before the farm one reaches the corner of a road. Go right, up hill, on this about 500 yds to reach the Walton Hill road. Cross over and go left onto footpath one started out on. After ½ mile, first just N, and then just S of the road, one returns past the orientation table to the Walton Hill car park.

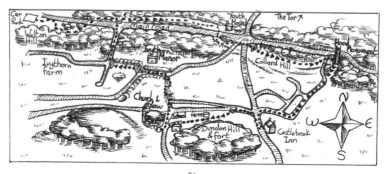

GLASTONBURY WALK VI - 1 MILE
A circuit of Glastonbury's Alehouses

It is not suggested that one drinks a pint of ale at each of the twelve pubs listed here, but – maybe – at some. Or else select part of this circuit. Start at (1) Becket's in the upper High Street and then go up the street a little to (2) Ye Queen's Head on the other side. Now proceed down the High Street to (3) the George & Pilgrims on the right. Easy to linger there, but continue to (4) The Crown, also known as 'The Backpackers'. Round the corner by the Market Cross to (5) the King William, in Market Place. Left out of the King Billy into Northload Street, where (6) Hawthorns Hotel (with bar and restaurant) is on the right. Next, across the street a little further, is the attractive (7) 'Who'd A Thought It'.

Go towards the car park on the west side of the 'Who'd A' and very shortly go through a

passage on one's left. This leads directly to (8) the Mitre Inn in Benedict Street. From there, exit left past St Benedict's Church until one reaches (9) the King Arthur on the same side. After the Arthur go back up by the church and turn right into St Benedict's Close. Then turn left towards the Abbey and come to Magdalene Street, where (10) Market House is just along to the left. Go right out of there and further along the street on the left is (11) The Globe. Left from the Globe and left round the corner into Bere Lane. At the top of Bere Lane and just round to the right in Chilkwell Street is (12) the Rifleman's Arms, our last port of call, which happens to have a late licence. (To return to the beginning, walk north on Chilkwell St and left back into the High Street.)

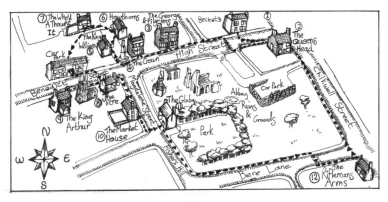

TIMELINE

3800 BC	Earliest Neolithic trackways across the Avalon Marshes
300 BC	Glastonbury Lake Village.
23 AD	Jesus Christ supposedly visits Glastonbury with St Joseph.
63	Supposed date of St Joseph of Arimathea's wattle church.
433	St Patrick comes to Glastonbury.
542	Geoffrey de Monmouth's date for death of King Arthur.
80~	St David Abbot. The wattle hut enclosed by wooden church?
597	St Augustine's mission from Rome to convert Anglo-Saxons.
940-56	St Dunstan is Abbot. The monastery prospers.
1184	Great Fire destroys Old Church and much of the Abbey.
1186	New St Mary Chapel complete. Work on Great Abbey begins.
1191	Monks claim discovery of the tomb of Arthur and Guinevere.
1275	Earthquake causes collapse of 1st St Michael's Church on Tor.
1278	Great Abbey Church complete. King Arthur reburied within.
1325~	Abbot Adam of Sodbury builds 2nd St Michael's on the Tor.
1465	Abbot Selwood builds St John's Ch. and George & Pilgrims.
1525-39	Richard Whiting is last Abbot. He completes Edgar Chapel.
1539	Henry VIII dissolves monasteries. Whiting executed on Tor.
1909-22	Bligh Bond's excavations. Revelations & dismissal by C. of E.
1969	John Michell reveals existence of the St Michael alignment.